BODRUM TRAVEL GUIDE 2024

Dive into Bodrum: A First-Timer's Guide to Sun-Kissed Paradise

JOSE D. GILLIAM

Copyright © 2024 by Jose D. Gilliam

All rights reserved. No part of this publication may be reproduced, distributed, or transmitted in any form or by any means, including photocopying, recording, or other electronic or mechanical methods, without the prior written permission of the publisher.

TABLE OF CONTENT

TABLE OF CONTENT..3
INTRODUCTION...7
   Welcome to Bodrum.. 7
   Bodrum: Where Turquoise Dreams Meet Sun-Kissed History..9
   Why Visit in 2024?.. 11
CHAPTER 1:
GETTING STARTED..**14**
   Travel Planning Tips.. 14
   Best Time to Visit... 16
   Navigating the Visa Maze: Entry Requirements for Bodrum... 18
   Travel Essentials & Insurance................................ 20
   Local Customs and Etiquette.................................23
   How to Get There: Airports, Transportation Options, and Arrival Tips..26
CHAPTER 2:
NAVIGATING BODRUM.. **29**
   Overview Map..29
   Public Transportation...31
   Renting a Car or Scooter.. 34
   Walking Tours.. 37
CHAPTER 3:
3-DAY TAILORED ITINERARIES FOR DIFFERENT TRAVELERS.. **40**
   History Enthusiast's Delight.................................... 40
   Sun, Sand, Sea Lovers...41

    Cultural Connoisseur's Journey................................42
    Adventure Seekers' Expedition...............................43

CHAPTER 4:
HISTORICAL TREASURES... 45
    Journey through Bodrum's Past............................. 45
    Unveiling Bodrum's Antiquities.............................. 47

CHAPTER 5:
CULTURAL DELIGHTS... 49
    Dive into History and Ancient Splendor.................. 49
    Bodrum Beyond the Beach....................................51

CHAPTER 6:
BODRUM'S BEACH BLISS: SUNSHINE, SAND, AND SECRET COVES.. 54
    Top Beaches for Every Vibe................................... 54
    Water Sports for the Thrill Seekers:........................55
    Hidden Coves for Paradise Hunters....................... 56

CHAPTER 7:
GASTRONOMIC ADVENTURES............................... 58
    Bodrum Bonanza: A Gastronomic Adventure for First-Timers..58
    Best Local Restaurants..61

CHAPTER 8:
VIBRANT NIGHTLIFE..64
    Bodrum Beats: Nightlife Hotspots for First-Timers. 64
    Bodrum After Dark: Dazzling Night Markets and Bustling Bazaars..66

CHAPTER 9:
WELLNESS AND RELAXATION............................... 68
    Bodrum Bliss: Unwind and Rejuvenate................. 68

Bodrum Bliss: Unwind at Top Wellness Resorts for First-Timers..70

CHAPTER 10:
DAY TRIPS AND EXCURSIONS..................72
Ephesus Day Trip & Pamukkale Excursion............72
Island Hopping & Nature's Enchantment................73

CHAPTER 11:
SHOPPING EXTRAVAGANZA........................75
Bodrum Bazaar Bonanza: Shopping Tips for Treasure Hunters..75
Bodrum Boutique Bonanza: Chic Shopping Districts for First-Timers... 76

CHAPTER 12:
ACCOMMODATION GUIDE.............................78
Bodrum Luxury Retreats: Sun-Kissed Splendor for First-Time Visitors...78
Bodrum Budget Bonanza: Cozy Stays without Breaking the Bank... 80
Bodrum Beyond the Ordinary: Unique Airbnb Stays for First-Timers.. 82

CHAPTER 13:
LOCAL TIPS AND INSIGHTS......................... 85
Insider Recommendations..85
Off-the-Beaten-Path Experiences............................88
Bodrum Babble: Cracking the Language Code for First-Timers...92

CHAPTER 14:
PRACTICAL INFORMATION..........................95
Emergency Contacts.. 95
Health and Safety Tips... 97

<u>5</u>

Money Matters..98
Communication Essentials.................................. 100
CONCLUSION.. 104
Recap of Bodrum's Charm.................................. 104
Encouragement for Future Travelers.................... 105
APPENDICES... 107
Useful Phrases in Turkish..................................... 107
Additional Resources..108

INTRODUCTION

Welcome to Bodrum

Welcome to Bodrum, a utopia of turquoise sunrises melting into sapphire twilights, a symphony of the Aegean where history whispers from old stones and laughter tumbles like bougainvillea blooms from whitewashed balconies. My first contact with this Turkish beauty was less of an arrival and more of a plunge. Not, mind you, the beautiful swan dive I'd envisioned, but a flailing belly flop into the cerulean embrace of the Aegean, courtesy of a rogue wave and a lost sandal.

Spitting seawater and grasping my dignity (and what remained of my sandal), I surfaced to the beautiful peals of laughter from a nearby gulet, its sails billowing like crimson dreams against the declining sun. In that moment, under the salty spray and the infectious pleasure, I knew Bodrum wasn't just a place; it was a mood. A sensation of sun-kissed skin and wind-tangled hair, of lingering mezze platters and glasses clinking with laughter under starlit skies.

My days were a tapestry made from the golden threads of discovery. I traversed the intricate alleyways of Bodrum Castle, where time itself seemed to echo in the worn ramparts and sun-bleached stones. I haggled for treasures in the lively market, falling to the mesmerizing chant of vendors and the rainbow of spices and silks. And, oh, the food! Each meal was a revelation, a symphony of tastes dancing on my tongue — melt-in-your-mouth dolmas, luscious kofte sizzling on charcoal barbecues, unbelievably fresh fish coated with lemon and olive oil.

But Bodrum wasn't just about hedonism. It was about adventure, about reaching beyond the horizon. I sailed aboard traditional wooden gulets, the wind whipping through my hair as we chased dolphins and plunged into hidden coves, the Aegean's cool embrace washing away the concerns of the world. I hiked through fragrant pine forests, their emerald depths tinted with sunlight, and stumbled across ancient ruins where moss-covered stones murmured tales of forgotten empires.

As the days bled into twilight, Bodrum changed into a kaleidoscope of colorful vitality. Rooftop bars thrummed with the pulse of DJs, their beats blending with the calm susurrus of the waves. Laughter streamed from tavernas like spilled wine, each clinking glass a toast to newfound friendships and stories exchanged under the watchful gaze of a star-studded sky.

But as intriguing as Bodrum's nightlife is, its true magic resides in the calm moments. Sunrise strolls along the beach, the sand cold beneath your feet and the sky ablaze with fiery hues. Late-night swims under a Milky Way carpet, the water a brilliant hug. These are the moments that endure long after your tan fades, the murmurs of a place that digs deep into your spirit.

So, dear tourist, if you seek a tapestry woven with history and joy, adventure and pleasure, look no further than Bodrum. Let its sun-drenched shores embrace you, its turquoise waters transport your concerns away, and its energetic energy inspire your wanderlust. Just remember, take your bikini, your dancing shoes, and an open heart. Bodrum is eager to weave its magic on you.

Bodrum: Where Turquoise Dreams Meet Sun-Kissed History

Imagine cobblestone walkways decorated with bougainvillea blooms, their vivid hues mirrored in the Aegean's dazzling embrace. Picture ancient castles standing sentry, narrating tales of vanished empires, while yachts bob like carefree butterflies on cerulean waters. This, my friend, is Bodrum - a Turkish jewel where history dances with hedonism, and days melt into sunsets like sweet honey.

Sunsets and Sunken Cities:
Dive into the Aegean's cold caress, chasing dolphins on a traditional gulet or snorkeling through underwater realms where sunken cities lie. Hike sun-drenched slopes to stumble upon lost temples, their aged stones testifying of ancient gods and forgotten prayers. As the sky explodes with the fiery breath of sunset, envision yourself on a rooftop bar, clinking glasses and weaving stories under a canopy of stars.

From Cleopatra's Kisses to Bazaar Bartering:
Bodrum murmurs of legendary loves. Queen Artemisia's resistance still rings in the wind, while stories of Cleopatra's secret rendezvous with Mark Antony linger in the salty air. Lose yourself in the labyrinthine lanes of the bazaar, bartering for treasures with a smile and a sparkle in your eye. Turkish delight will melt on your lips, spices will seduce your senses, and silk scarves will whisper promises of clandestine kisses under the Aegean moon.

More Than Just Beach Bliss:
Bodrum isn't just a playground for sun-seekers. History aficionados will immerse themselves in the Bodrum Museum of Underwater Archaeology, where shipwrecked artifacts tell tales of marine exploits. Art lovers will be attracted by the ancient Greek

amphitheater, where modern performances bring classic legends to life. And foodies? Well, ready for a culinary voyage, from melt-in-your-mouth dolmas to exquisite fish sprinkled with lemon and olive oil.

So, dear traveler, bring your dancing shoes, an open heart, and a zest for adventure. Bodrum awaits, ready to weave its charm on you.

Bonus Tip: Skip the tourist traps and sail away to the picturesque fishing village of Gümüşlük, where time dances to the rhythm of the waves and delicious seafood reigns supreme.

Come, let Bodrum paint your spirit with sunshine and fill your heart with the whispers of history. This Aegean paradise is begging to be discovered.

Why Visit in 2024?

Ditch the predictable, dear. 2024 calls for Bodrum, Aegean siren with a twist. Forget Santorini's whitewashed whispers; Bodrum hums with a lively pulse. Think yachts mingling with gulets, ancient ruins winking at rooftop bars, and history-kissed coves calling for your dive. Here's why you need Bodrum this year:

Sun-kissed history that rocks: Dive beneath shipwrecks at the Underwater Archaeology Museum, then clink glasses under Bodrum Castle's watchful gaze. This ain't your dusty textbook history; it's in the air you breathe, the waters you swim in.

Hedonism with a conscience: Luxury beach clubs meet picturesque villages where sustainability drinks cocktails with you. Think yoga flows on private coves, followed by mezze feasts under starlit sky. Bodrum's got your cold and your thrill covered.

Beyond the beach (but still beachy, obvs): Hike aromatic pine forests, stumble upon forgotten temples, and sail the Aegean aboard traditional wooden gulets. This ain't simply sandcastles and sunburns; Bodrum's an explorer's playground.

A touch of the unexpected: Dive into the thriving cultural scene, from contemporary galleries to ancient amphitheater performances. Bodrum's got more layers than an Ottoman onion (and just as delicious).

2024's secret sauce: New boutique hotels are cropping up, hidden coves are being uncovered, and the party scene is hotter than ever. You'll be the first to notify your friends: "Bodrum? It's the next big thing."

So, pack your dancing shoes, a bargaining spirit, and your appetite for Aegean adventures. Bodrum's 2024 symphony awaits, played on sun-kissed coasts and murmured by ancient stones. Be there, or be square (and frankly, a little sun-deprived).

CHAPTER 1:

GETTING STARTED

Travel Planning Tips

Plan Your Dream Escape:

Seasonality is Key: Summer (June-August) is peak season, with searing sun and a lively throng. Consider the shoulder seasons (April-May, September-October) for good weather and acceptable tourist numbers.

Visa & Entry: Most nationalities do not require visas for short-term stays (see official sources). Bring your passport and proof of onward travel.

Travel Essentials: Pack lightweight, breathable clothing, a hat, sunscreen, and comfortable shoes. Pack a bikini for the beach and a scarf for cultural attractions. Consider using a Turkish phrasebook for basic conversation.

Travel Insurance: Protect yourself with comprehensive travel insurance that includes medical emergencies, trip cancellations, and lost luggage.

Budgeting Tip:

Accommodation: Select your stay based on your preferences: luxurious resorts, low-cost hotels, or unique Airbnbs. For a worry-free vacation, look into all-inclusive packages.

Transportation: Public transportation is dependable and inexpensive. Taxis are frequently available; however, fares must be agreed upon in advance. Consider renting a car to explore further.

Food: Try street food for cheap snacks or eat great dinners at local restaurants. Haggling is allowed at markets and bazaars.

Pro Tip for Newcomers:

-Download the "Muvat" app to easily translate menus, signs, and basic conversations.

Embrace the local money: Download a currency converter app and bring some Turkish Lira (TRY) for little transactions.

Learn some basic Turkish: "Merhaba" (hello), "Teşekkür ederim" (thank you), and "Ne kadar?" (how much?) will get you a long way.

Respect the local customs: Dress conservatively when visiting religious locations. Be aware of prayer times and noise levels.

Note: This is only a starting point. With careful planning and an open mind, you're ready for a memorable Bodrum journey!

Best Time to Visit

The greatest time to visit Bodrum depends on what you prioritize in your holiday! Here's a breakdown:

Sunshine Seekers (June-September):

Highlights: Hottest weather (30°C+), great for sunbathing and swimming, vibrant atmosphere, long days with plenty of sunshine.
Downsides: Crowded beaches, higher pricing, potentially uncomfortable heat, increased tourist traffic.

Shoulder Seasons (April-May, October-November):

Highlights: Pleasant temperatures (20-25°C), fewer crowds, reduced rates, still ideal for swimming, chance to discover cultural attractions without the summer heat.
Downsides: Some amenities and businesses may have limited hours, weather can be unpredictable with a potential of rain.

Budget Travelers (October-March):

Highlights: Lowest rates, fewer crowds, quieter environment, chance to experience local life, perfect for seeing historical sites.

Downsides: Some businesses and attractions may be closed, cooler weather may not be suitable for swimming, occasional rain showers.

Alternative Options:

September: Warmest water temperatures, excellent for swimming and diving.
May: Bicycle Festival with vibrant events and performances.
Autumn: Vibrant fall foliage in the neighboring mountains.

Note: These are only broad suggestions. Bodrum's weather can be unpredictable, so always check the forecast before arranging your vacation.

My recommendations:
- If you want the perfect beach holiday with hot weather and vibrant nightlife, select June-September.
- For a balance of pleasant weather, fewer crowds, and good value, aim for April-May or October-November.
- If you're on a tight budget or prefer a quieter experience, consider October-March.

Ultimately, the best time to visit Bodrum is whenever it best meets your unique preferences and priorities. Do your homework, set your dates, and be ready for an incredible Turkish vacation!

Navigating the Visa Maze: Entry Requirements for Bodrum

Welcome, first-time traveler, to the wonderful world of Bodrum! Before you pack your swimwear and bargain for spices in the bazaar, let's solve the visa question so your arrival is seamless as Aegean sunshine.

Good News: Most travelers don't require a visa to enter Turkey for stays up to 90 days, including popular nationalities like Americans, Canadians, Australians, and Europeans. Phew, right? Just double-check with your home country's embassy to determine if you're part of the lucky visa-free club.

For those who DO need a visa:

e-Visa: The easiest and most economical alternative! Apply online at least two days before your trip on the official Turkish e-Visa website [https://www.evisa.gov.tr/].

It costs roughly USD 60-80 depending on your nationality, and you'll get your result within 24 hours (typically much faster). Print your e-Visa acceptance email and keep it available at the border.

Regular Visa: If your country isn't qualified for an e-Visa, you'll need to apply at the nearest Turkish embassy or consulate. Expect longer processing periods (one to two weeks) and higher expenses (up to USD 150).

Tips for First-Timers:
Double-check your passport validity: You need at least 6 months of validity remaining from your admission date.
Carry proof of onward travel: Show airline tickets or confirmation for another exit from Turkey to avoid any obstacles.
Have sufficient funds: Demonstrate proof of enough money for your stay (about USD 50 per day) to prevent unwanted questions.
Download the "Cimer" app: This official Turkish app interprets emergency announcements and gives valuable information.
Relax and smile: Border personnel are used to welcome visitors. Be polite, display your paperwork confidently, and you'll be basking on Bodrum beaches in no time!

Bonus Tip: Skip the huge waits at the airport immigration by utilizing online e-Gates if accessible for your country.

Remember, visa requirements might vary, so always check the latest information with your country's embassy or the official Turkish e-Visa website before confirming your travel plans. Now, with this visa knowledge in your back pocket, you're set to attack Bodrum! Get ready for turquoise waters, ancient wonders, and a taste of Turkish charm. Happy travels!

Travel Essentials & Insurance

The attraction of Bodrum beckons, and you're geared yourself for adventure! Now comes the key step: ensuring you're equipped for sun-drenched days and unexpected situations. Let's look into travel needs and insurance, your dependable friends on this Aegean escapade.

Travel Essentials:

Clothing:
- Versatile, quick-drying clothes for warm weather: sundresses, t-shirts, shorts, lightweight pants, swimwear.

- Comfortable walking shoes and sandals for exploring towns and the beach.
- Consider a sunhat, sunglasses, and a light scarf for windy days.
- Don't forget dressier clothing for a nice restaurant or rooftop bar.

Essentials:
- Sunscreen and moisturizer (SPF 30+ suggested)
- Travel adaptor and portable charger
- First-aid kit with basic meds
- Reusable water bottle (keep hydrated under the Turkish sun!)
- Photocopies of your passport and other documents
- Phrasebook with typical Turkish words (extra points for cultural awareness!)

Optional Extras:
- Waterproof pocket for phone and valuables
- Quick-drying travel towel
- Book or Kindle for those leisurely beach afternoons
- Camera or phone with ample capacity to capture every Bodrum moment

Insurance:
Travel insurance isn't just for hypochondriacs. It provides peace of mind and financial security against unanticipated events like:

- Trip cancellation or interruption due to illness, injury, or weather
- Medical emergency while abroad
- Lost or damaged luggage
- Flight delays or cancellations

Bodrum-Specific Considerations:
- Consider insurance that covers adventure activities like diving or sailing.
- Some insurance may not cover pre-existing medical issues, so check carefully.
- Choose a plan with comprehensive medical coverage, especially if you rely on specific prescriptions.

Tips for Finding the Right Insurance:
- Compare quotes from several suppliers and study the tiny print.
- Choose a plan that suits your budget and vacation activities.
- Don't wait until the last minute to get insured.

Note: Packing the correct gear and having suitable insurance will ensure a hassle-free and safe journey to Bodrum. So, pack your things, guarantee your peace of mind, and conquer the Aegean heat with confidence!

Bonus Tip: Download your travel insurance provider's app for convenient access to policy data and emergency support.

Now, off you go, armed with information and essentials! Dive into Bodrum's turquoise waves, walk amid ancient ruins, and taste the vibrant city life. Bon journey!

Local Customs and Etiquette

Bodrum beckons with its sun-kissed shores and dynamic energy, but learning local customs can enrich your experience and avoid any unintended faux pas. Fear not, first-time traveler! Here's your crash course on navigating the friendly currents of Turkish hospitality:

Greetings:
- A warm handshake and a smile are always appreciated.
- When addressing seniors, use "amca" (uncle) or "teyze" (aunt) with their names. - Women generally greet women with a kiss on the cheek.

Dress Code:
- While Bodrum is more relaxed than certain places of Turkey, avoid revealing apparel at religious sites or conservative villages.

- Respectful clothing at mosques is necessary for both men and women. For ladies, cover your head and shoulders, and wear longer skirts or pants. Men should keep their knees covered.
- In restaurants and bars, smart casual dress is often acceptable.

Dining Etiquette:
- Meals are a social affair, so enjoy leisurely lunches and dinners.
- Don't be shocked if food arrives in stages, savor each course!
- Bread is a mainstay - use it to scoop up delectable dips.
- Tipping is not requested, although a little gratuity for good service is appreciated.

Social Interactions:
- Direct eye contact is a sign of respect.
- Avoid highly personal issues in initial conversations.
- Public shows of affection are generally not frowned upon, but keep it within appropriate limits.
- When welcomed to someone's home, bring a small present, such as cookies or flowers.

General Courtesy:
- Remove your shoes when visiting mosques and some homes.

- Smoking is common in outdoor settings, however be aware of non-smokers.
- Bargaining is anticipated in bazaars, have fun with it!
- Learn a few basic Turkish phrases like "teşekkür ederim" (thank you) and "merhaba" (hello).

Bonus Tips for First-Timers:
- Carry small coins for taxis and tips.
- Download a Turkish translation software for handy communication.
- Be patient and understanding, things may not always proceed at a western pace.
- Embrace the opportunity to learn and participate in local customs.

No, cultural sensitivity is crucial to creating strong connections. By demonstrating respect for local customs, you'll open yourself up to a better understanding of the Turkish way of life and create lasting experiences in Bodrum. So, dive into the turquoise waves, lose yourself in the labyrinthine market, and taste the warmth of Turkish hospitality.

How to Get There: Airports, Transportation Options, and Arrival Tips

Getting to Bodrum, the jewel of the Aegean, shouldn't be a grueling obstacle course. But navigating airports, transportation options, and arrival logistics can be difficult for first-timers. Fear not, explorer! This book is your compass to a smooth landing and a seamless start to your Turkish experience.

Airports:

Your entrance to Bodrum depends on your budget and travel preferences:

Milas-Bodrum Airport (BJV): The nearest and most convenient alternative, about 35km from Bodrum. Expect hassle-free arrival with plenty of transportation alternatives and competitive airfare pricing. Ideal for most travelers.

Dalaman Airport (DLM): Located further away (180km), Dalaman might provide cheaper flights, especially during off-season. Be prepared for longer transfer times (about 2-3 hours) or higher taxi rates. Consider this option if budget is a key factor and you don't mind the extra travel time.

Transportation Options:
Once you land, choose your chariot to Bodrum:

Taxis: The quickest and most pleasant choice, immediately available outside the arrivals hall. Negotiate fares upfront, especially for unmetered taxis. Expect to pay roughly €30-€50 for the trip to Bodrum town.

Havaş Shuttles: Shared buses delivering budget-friendly journeys to Bodrum and other destinations. Look for the orange buses outside the terminal. Cost roughly €15-€20 per person.

Pre-Booked Transfers: Arrange private transports with your hotel or local providers for a seamless and stress-free arrival, especially if you're traveling with family or bags. Expect charges to range from €40-€80 depending on the car and distance.

Car Rental: Rent a car at the airport for independent exploring (recommended for experienced drivers). Consider traffic and restricted parking in Bodrum town. Rental fees vary depending on season and size of car.

Arrival Tips:
Visa Check: Double-check visa requirements and have your paperwork readily accessible.

Currency Exchange: Change some money at the airport for initial expenses like cabs or refreshments. ATMs are extensively available in Bodrum.

Mobile Data: Purchase a local SIM card for internet access and communication. Consider pre-ordering one online for easier setup.

Offline Maps: Download offline maps to save data consumption, especially beneficial if utilizing shared shuttles or taxis.

Accommodation Details: Have your hotel address accessible for faster transfers.

Relax and Enjoy: You've arrived in heaven! Breathe in the Aegean air and get ready for an incredible adventure.

Pricing Rundown:
Taxis: €30-€50
Havaş Shuttles: €15-€20
Pre-Booked Transfers: €40-€80
Car Rental: Variable according on season and vehicle size

CHAPTER 2:

NAVIGATING BODRUM

Overview Map

Embark on a smooth journey of Bodrum with our complete overview map, meant to be your reliable companion in traversing this charming peninsula.

Highlights:
1. Historical Landmarks:

Bodrum Castle: A spectacular stronghold guarding the shoreline, affording panoramic views of the city and the Aegean Sea.

Mausoleum at Halicarnassus: Uncover the vestiges of one of the Seven Wonders of the Ancient World, a tribute to Bodrum's rich history.

Old Theater of Bodrum: Immerse yourself in the grandeur of this old amphitheater, echoing tales of plays from years ago.

2. Cultural Hotspots:

Bodrum Museum of Underwater Archaeology: Delve into the nautical history of Bodrum, exhibiting items from sunken ships and historic treasures.
Bodrum Amphitheater: Witness live performances in a beautiful setting, merging history with contemporary entertainment.
Bodrum Maritime Museum: Explore the maritime heritage of the region through displays showing traditional boats and seafaring culture.

3. Scenic Beaches:

Zeki Müren Arts Museum Beach: A calm hideaway with golden sands, named after the legendary Turkish singer, Zeki Müren.
Bitez Beach: Embrace the laid-back environment and turquoise waves, excellent for sunbathing and water sports.
Gümbet Beach: Known for its active nightlife, this beach offers a combination of daytime relaxation and evening activities.

4. Dining and Shopping Districts:

Oasis Shopping District: A fashionable enclave near Bodrum Marina, boasting fashion-forward retailers and trendy eateries.

Grand Bazaar: Navigate the small passageways filled with vendors providing anything from spices and linens to handcrafted trinkets.

Navigational Tips:
Landmarks as Anchors: Use historical landmarks as reference points when investigating. The castle, amphitheater, and museums operate as anchors for numerous districts.
Public Transportation Hubs: Identify important transportation hubs for easy access to different sections of Bodrum.

Local Streets and Alleys: Don't hesitate to venture off the beaten path. Some of Bodrum's best finds are buried in the picturesque lanes and alleys.

This overview map is your gateway to a seamless Bodrum experience, ensuring you don't miss any of the engaging features that make this location a treasure trove for holidaymakers. Explore with confidence and let the map uncover the wonders of Bodrum at your own leisure.

Public Transportation

1. Buses:

Bodrum has a well-organized public bus system connecting various neighborhoods and nearby towns.

Fares: Bus fares typically range from 5 to 10 Turkish Lira. Prices may vary depending on the distance traveled.

Payment: Pay in cash directly to the driver upon boarding. Have smaller denominations for convenience.

2. Dolmuş (Minibuses):

Availability: Dolmuş vehicles are a popular means of transportation, operating on fixed routes and offering a cost-effective option.

Fares: Fares range from 3 to 10 Turkish Lira per person. Payment is made in cash to the driver.

Tips: Hail Dolmuş from the roadside, and locals are usually helpful in identifying the right one for your destination.

3. Boats and Ferries:

Coastal Routes: Bodrum's coastal areas offer boat services connecting different points, including nearby islands.

Fares: Boat fares vary based on the destination. Short trips may cost around 15-20 Turkish Lira.

Schedule: Check schedules at the departure points, as they may be subject to changes.

4. Taxi Services:

Availability: Taxis are readily available throughout Bodrum, with stands at key locations and easily hailed on the streets.

Fares: Taxis typically have meters. Short intra-city rides may cost 10-20 Turkish Lira.

Payment: Cash is the preferred method. Confirm if the taxi has a meter before starting your journey.

5. Walking Tours:

Guided Tours: Various companies offer guided walking tours to explore historical sites and hidden gems. Prices range from 50 to 100 Turkish Lira per person.

Self-Guided Strolls: Bodrum's Old Town is perfect for self-guided walks. Wear comfortable shoes for cobbled streets.

6. Transportation Apps:

Ride-Hailing Apps: Utilize ride-hailing apps for convenient taxi services. Ensure you have a reliable internet connection.

Navigation Apps: Apps like Google Maps provide real-time information on bus routes, schedules, and walking directions.

COVID-19 Considerations:

Mask Mandate: Follow any mask mandates in public transportation. Masks may be required on buses, boats, and in taxis.

Sanitization: Practice good hand hygiene. Carry hand sanitizer and use it after using public transportation.

Local Tips for Travelers:
Plan Routes in Advance: Use navigation apps to plan your routes and check for any updates on schedules.
Ask Locals: Don't hesitate to ask locals for guidance or recommendations on the best transportation options.

Stay updated on local guidelines, schedules, and any changes in public transportation to ensure a smooth and safe exploration of Bodrum.

Renting a Car or Scooter

1. Renting an automobile:
Rental firms: Numerous automobile rental firms operate in Bodrum, both at the airport and in the city center.

Requirements:
Valid Driver's License: A valid international or local driver's license is essential.
Passport: Have a valid passport for identification.
Age Requirements: Minimum age requirements for hiring a car normally range from 21 to 25, depending on the rental operator.

Costs:
- Daily charges start at roughly 150 Turkish Lira, varying based on the vehicle type, rental duration, and insurance coverage.
- Additional costs may include fuel, tolls, and parking fees.

Tips:
- Check the vehicle completely for any damages before accepting it.
- Familiarize yourself with local traffic rules and road signage.
- Consider renting a GPS for navigating.

2. **Renting a Scooter**:

Rental Shops: Scooter rental shops are abundant in Bodrum, especially in tourist districts and near major attractions.

Requirements:

Valid Driver's License: A valid international or local driver's license is normally necessary.

Passport: Have a valid passport for identification.

Age restrictions: Minimum age restrictions for hiring a scooter vary but are commonly around 18 to 21.

Costs

- Daily rental fees for scooters can range from 50 to 100 Turkish Lira, depending on the model of scooter and rental duration.
- Fuel expenditures are negligible for scooters.

Tips:
- Wear a helmet, which is necessary for both safety and legal reasons.
- Be cautious on the roadways, especially in busy places.

COVID-19 Considerations:
Sanitization: Ensure that the rental vehicle or scooter is fully sterilized before use.
Safety Measures: Follow any additional safety measures adopted by the rental agencies, such as contactless transactions or disinfection protocols.

Local Tips for Renters:
Negotiation: If renting for a prolonged period, inquire about potential reductions or package deals.
Parking: Familiarize yourself with parking restrictions and available parking spots in Bodrum.
Traffic Patterns: Be aware of traffic patterns, especially during peak hours.

Environmental Considerations:

Eco-Friendly Options: Some rental firms offer eco-friendly or electric scooters, helping with sustainability efforts.

By complying to local restrictions, being aware of traffic conditions, and taking required safety precautions, renting a car or scooter in Bodrum can offer you the flexibility to explore this wonderful place at your own leisure.

Walking Tours

1. Guided Walking Tours:
Options: Several local tour companies provide guided walking tours, providing insights into Bodrum's rich history and culture.

Themes: Tours may focus on historical landmarks, archaeological sites, or specific topics like gastronomy or art tours.

Duration: Guided walking tours normally take 2 to 3 hours, allowing a full yet reasonable overview.

2. Self-Guided Strolls:

Old Town Exploration: Bodrum's Old Town (Kaleiçi) is an excellent destination for self-guided treks. Wander through lovely small lanes and discover hidden jewels.

Historical Sites: Create your plan to tour historical places including Bodrum Castle, the Amphitheatre, and the Mausoleum of Halicarnassus on foot.

Local Markets: Walk around local markets like Bodrum Bazaar to experience the vibrant atmosphere and browse for souvenirs.

3. Walking Apps and Maps:
Navigation Apps: Use navigation apps like Google Maps for real-time directions and to explore sites of interest.

Offline Maps: Download offline maps to traverse locations with restricted internet connectivity.

Walking Tour applications: Explore walking tour applications built for individual sites, giving audio tours and historical information.

4. Cultural Districts:
Marina District: Take a leisurely stroll around the waterfront, lined with restaurants, cafes, and stores. Enjoy the magnificent views of yachts and the castle.

Arts and Crafts Street:.Visit Cumhuriyet Street, noted for its arts and crafts boutiques. Experience the local art scene and perhaps purchase unique handmade products.

5. COVID-19 Considerations:
Group Size: Check for latest information on group sizes for guided tours, conforming to any social distancing rules.
Mask Usage: Be aware of any local mandates regarding mask usage, especially in busy areas or indoor attractions.

Local Tips for Walkers:
Comfortable Footwear: Wear comfortable shoes ideal for walking on both cobblestone streets and uneven terrain.
Water and Sunscreen: Carry a bottle of water and apply sunscreen, especially during warmer months.
Exploration Time: Allocate extra time for unplanned discoveries and interactions with locals.

Environmental Considerations:
Respect Local Culture: Be attentive of local customs and cultural practices during your walks.
Waste Reduction: Consider bringing a reusable water bottle to minimize plastic waste.

CHAPTER 3:

3-DAY TAILORED ITINERARIES FOR DIFFERENT TRAVELERS

History Enthusiast's Delight

Day 1: Ancient Wonders Exploration
Morning: Begin at Bodrum Castle, home of the Museum of Underwater Archaeology. Engage in a guided tour for in-depth knowledge.
Afternoon: Visit the Mausoleum of Halicarnassus, one of the Seven Wonders of the Ancient World. Explore the full information and historical context.
Evening: Stroll through Bodrum's Old Town, enjoying old ruins and historical structures. Immerse yourself in the wonderful surroundings.

Day 2: Ancient Theaters and Museums
Morning: Explore the majesty of Bodrum Amphitheatre. Imagine the concerts that once graced this famous theater.
Afternoon: Dive into the interesting artifacts of the Bodrum Museum of History and Art. Check for any temporary displays or recent archaeological findings.

Evening: Enjoy dinner in the evocative setting of the ancient theater, soaking in the historical aura.

Day 3: Day Trip to Ephesus
Tips: Opt for a guided tour of Ephesus, exposing the ancient city's mysteries. Witness the Library of Celsus and other notable structures.

Note: Stay updated on travel advisories and assure a seamless day trip with reliable transit choices.

Sun, Sand, Sea Lovers

Day 1: Beach Day Bliss
Morning: Relax at Bodrum's popular beaches like Camel Beach or Bitez Beach. Soak up the sun and plan beach activities.
Afternoon: Engage in watersports or simply bask in the sun. Check for beachfront services and amenities.
Evening: Choose a coastal restaurant for a nice supper with beautiful sea views.

Day 2: Boat Excursion
Tips: Book a full-day boat excursion visiting peaceful coves and snorkeling areas. Ensure the boat is equipped for a comfortable cruise.

Note: Be prepared with essentials like sunscreen, caps, and swimsuits for a day of water enjoyment.

Day 3: Island Hopping
Tips: Plan a day of island exploration, seeing adjacent beauties like Karaada or Kos. Check ferry schedules for hassle-free island hopping.

Note: Verify weather conditions and ensure a smooth island-hopping vacation, discovering the individual appeal of each site.

Cultural Connoisseur's Journey

Day 1: Arts and Heritage Exploration
Morning: Stroll down Cumhuriyet Street, known for its arts and crafts enterprises. Engage with local craftsmen and explore their creative process.
Afternoon: Visit local galleries displaying contemporary and traditional Turkish art. Take time to admire the diverse artistic expressions.
Evening: Attend a cultural show or live music event. Immerse yourself in the local artistic scene and engage with fellow fans.

Day 2: Culinary Exploration
Morning: Participate in a cooking lesson to get into the complexities of Turkish cuisine. Learn about regional ingredients and cooking techniques.
Afternoon: Explore local markets for fresh produce and spices. Engage with vendors and receive insights into the culinary culture.
Evening: Indulge in a typical Turkish supper at a highly recognized restaurant. Savor the flavors of Bodrum's culinary pleasures.

Day 3: Architecture and Local Immersion
Morning: Explore old mosques, Ottoman-era architecture, and other cultural landmarks. Gain a greater knowledge of Bodrum's architectural history.
Afternoon: Wander around small settlements, seeing daily life and traditions. Connect with locals to enrich your cultural experience.

Tips: Respect local customs during mosque visits and dress modestly.

Adventure Seekers' Expedition

Day 1: Water Sports Extravaganza

Morning: Dive into the day with water sports like windsurfing or kiteboarding. Ensure safety measures are in place and brace up for an adrenaline-filled encounter.

Afternoon: Jet-skiing or parasailing adds excitement to the day. Negotiate pricing in advance and capture wonderful moments in the water.

Evening: Conclude the day with a seaside barbecue lunch, sharing adventure stories with fellow tourists.

Day 2: Off-Road Adventure

Morning: Embark on a full-day jeep safari, discovering Bodrum's rugged scenery and off-road paths. Capture breathtaking vistas and savor the thrill of the voyage.

Evening: Gather around a campfire for a lovely dinner under the sky, reliving the day's activities.

Tips: Wear comfortable clothing and pack a hat and sunglasses for the safari.

Day 3: Hiking and Paragliding

Tips: Wear sturdy hiking shoes and take a refillable water bottle.

Morning: Begin the day with a scenic hike to Bodrum's overlooks, affording panoramic vistas. Enjoy the serenity of nature.

Afternoon: Elevate the adventure with paragliding, soaring above the shoreline for a bird's-eye perspective. Capture the breathtaking panoramas from high above.

CHAPTER 4:

HISTORICAL TREASURES

Journey through Bodrum's Past

Bodrum Castle:
Location: Bodrum Kalesi, 48400 Bodrum/Muğla, Turkey
Highlights: Majestic medieval fortification overlooking the Aegean Sea, home to the Museum of Underwater Archaeology.
Tips: Explore the Knights of St. John exhibition, climb the towers for panoramic vistas, and delve into the interesting undersea items in the museum.

Pricing for Bodrum Castle:
Regular Ticket: ₺70 (Turkish Lira)
Students: ₺25 (with valid ID)
Free for Children: Under 12 years

Mausoleum at Halicarnassus:
Location: Tepecik Mahallesi, 48400 Bodrum/Muğla, Turkey

Highlights: Ancient tomb, one of the Seven Wonders of the Ancient World, embellished with beautiful sculptures and reliefs.
Tips: Admire the majesty of Mausolus's burial site, see the friezes and statues, and grasp the historical significance of this amazing structure.

Pricing for Mausoleum at Halicarnassus:
Regular Ticket: ₺40 (Turkish Lira)
Students: ₺15 (with valid ID)
Free for Children: Under 12 years

For First-Time Travelers:
Combined Tickets: Consider getting combined tickets for both sites for a cost-effective solution.
Guided Tours: Engage in guided tours to get deeper historical insights.
Photographing: Capture the detailed details but verify the guidelines for photographing in sensitive locations.
Cultural Context: Utilize on-site guides to grasp the historical and cultural relevance.
Timings: Plan your visit during daylight hours to properly enjoy the architectural marvels.

Set out on a thrilling trip through time as Bodrum Castle and the Mausoleum at Halicarnassus beckon you to investigate the echoes of past civilizations. With low pricing and rich historical tales, these locations promise an amazing experience for first-time guests in Bodrum.

Unveiling Bodrum's Antiquities

Ancient Theater of Bodrum:
Location: Üçler Sokak No:7, 48400 Bodrum/Muğla, Turkey
Highlights: Well-preserved ancient amphitheater with a seating capacity of 13,000, delivering outstanding acoustics.
Tips: Attend a live performance during the Bodrum Antique Theater Festival if your visit aligns. Enjoy panoramic views of Bodrum from this historic venue.

Pricing for Ancient Theater of Bodrum:
Regular Ticket: ₺25 (Turkish Lira)
Students: ₺10 (with valid ID)
Free for Children: Under 12 years

Myndos Gate:
Location: Just east of Bodrum city center, near Gumbet.
Highlights: Ancient city gate dating back to the 4th century BC, a vestige of the city walls.
Tips: Capture the historical significance of this key entry and explore the vestiges of the city walls.

Pricing for Myndos Gate:
No admission fee: Myndos Gate is often available without a special entrance fee.

For First-Time Travelers:
Guided Tours: Enhance your historical understanding with guided tours available at both sites.
Combination Tickets: Check for combination tickets offering admission to numerous historical sites in Bodrum.
Comfortable Attire: Wear comfortable shoes for exploring the theater, and consider a hat and sunscreen for outdoor trips.
Photography: Capture the antique beauty but be mindful of any laws governing photography.
Cultural Insights: Engage with local guides to obtain insights into the historical and cultural context of these outstanding sites.

Explore the echoes of antiquity as you step into the Ancient Theater of Bodrum and pass through the Myndos Gate, experiencing the rich history and architectural treasures that Bodrum has retained. With low cost and a richness of historical narratives, these locations promise a memorable adventure for first-time travelers in Bodrum.

CHAPTER 5:

CULTURAL DELIGHTS

Dive into History and Ancient Splendor

Bodrum isn't all about sun-kissed beaches and party scenes. Its rich past whispers from every stone, beckoning you to explore layers of interesting civilizations. Immerse yourself in these two cultural gems, must-visits for any first-time traveler:

Bodrum Museum of Underwater Archaeology:
Dive into the Depths: Discover the secrets of the Aegean Sea through shipwrecks spanning millennia. Witness amphoras, glassware, and daily artifacts that offer a vivid picture of ancient marine life.
Highlights: The Glass Hall's magnificent collection, the world's oldest shipwreck (Uluburun), and interactive exhibits bring history to life.

Practicalities:
Location: Bodrum Castle, Bodrum 48200, Turkey
Opening Hours: Summer (Apr-Oct): 8:30 AM - 7:30 PM, Winter (Nov-Mar): 8:30 AM - 5:00 PM (Closed Mondays)
 Admission Fee: 40 TRY (about $5 USD)

Website: [https://www.bodrum-museum.com/]
Phone Number: +90 252 414 17 96

Tips for First-Timers:
-Allocate at least 1-2 hours for your visit.
-Take the audio guide (English available) for deeper insights.
-Combine your visit with Bodrum Castle for a history double-whammy.
-Wear comfortable shoes and sun protection, as some parts are outdoors.

Bodrum Amphitheater:
Echoes of Antiquity: Step into the awe-inspiring 2nd-century Roman amphitheater, previously a platform for gladiatorial combats and theatrical plays. Imagine the noise of the crowds and the drama that occurred in this antique theater.
Breathtaking Views: Soak in panoramic sights of Bodrum Harbor and the Aegean Sea from the higher floors. Feel the history come alive as you imagine the bustling life during its prime.

Practicalities:
Location: İstiklal Caddesi, Bodrum 48200, Turkey
Opening Hours: Open daily, sunrise till sunset (Free Entry)
Admission Fee: Free (Donations welcome)

Website:
[https://muze.gov.tr/muze-detay?SectionId=BSA01&DistId=MRK]
Phone Number: +90 252 414 29 74

Tips for First-Timers:
-Visit after sunset for magnificent golden light and breathtaking views.
-Pack a hat and drink, as there is limited shade.
-Combine your visit with neighboring Bodrum Castle and the Museum of Underwater Archaeology.
-Respect the historical significance of the site and avoid climbing on structures.

These two cultural treasures offer a look into Bodrum's rich past, from ancient maritime trade to gladiatorial shows. So, dig into history, marvel at architectural masterpieces, and let your imagination create the scenes of life long past. Your Bodrum experience will be better and more gratifying with these cultural gems on your schedule!

Bodrum Beyond the Beach

While Bodrum's sun-kissed beaches and crystalline waters beckon, its cultural riches provide a deeper dive into history and local culture. Immerse yourself in the rich tapestry of Bodrum's soul with these must-see cultural delights:

Bodrum Maritime Museum:
Step into a world of naval history: This fascinating museum highlights Bodrum's maritime past, from ancient seafaring vessels to conventional wooden boats and fascinating archeological artifacts.
Explore interactive exhibits: Learn about sponge diving, boat construction, and the importance of the Aegean Sea in forming Bodrum's identity.
Admire remarkable collections: Get up close with miniature ships, marine gear, and magnificent seashells from around the world.

Details:
Website: [https://bodrumdenizmuzesi.org/]
Address: Bedesten Mahallesi, Neyzen Tevfik Sokağı No:8, 48400 Bodrum, Muğla, Turkey
Phone: +90 252 414 15 16
Pricing: 20 TRY (about $2.50 USD) for adults, free for children under 12

Local Festivals & Events:
Bodrum International Bodrum Short Film Festival (July): Immerse yourself in a world of independent cinema, short films, and workshops with internationally famous filmmakers.

International Bodrum Yacht Festival (October): Witness a brilliant display of luxury yachts, sailing boats, and marine festivities, with live music, exhibitions, and cultural events.

Gümüşlük Lantern Festival (August): Experience the wonderful sight of hundreds of brightly lit lanterns dazzling the night sky at the lovely village of Gümüşlük.

Bodrum International Folklore Festival (August): Immerse yourself in a spectacular festival of traditional music, dancing, and costumes from throughout the world.

Bonus Tips for First-Timers:

Purchase festival tickets in advance: Popular events can sell out quickly.

Dress comfortably: Be prepared for walking and standing for long periods.

Respect local customs: Dress modestly if attending religious ceremonies or events.

Learn a few basic Turkish phrases: A few "merhabas" (hellos) can go a long way!

Embrace the experience: Immerse yourself in the sights, sounds, and flavors of Bodrum's cultural tapestry.

Exploring Bodrum's cultural scene provides a special depth to your first-time trip. Step beyond the shore, dig into history and traditions, and let the liveliness of Bodrum's spirit captivate your heart.

CHAPTER 6:

BODRUM'S BEACH BLISS: SUNSHINE, SAND, AND SECRET COVES

Bodrum's coastline is a patchwork of sun-kissed beaches, each one giving a unique bit of heaven. From lively party strips to tranquil secluded coves, there's a perfect stretch of sand for every first-time adventurer. So, grab your bikini, slather on the sunscreen, and dive into these Bodrum beach beauties:

Top Beaches for Every Vibe

Gümüşlük Beach: Soak in the laid-back appeal of this crescent-shaped beach with stunning turquoise waves and charming wooden boats bobbing gently. Ideal for families and nature enthusiasts.
Address: Gümüşlük Mahallesi, Bodrum 48200, Turkey.
Pricing: Free access, with beach chair and umbrella rentals available.
Tip: Explore the lovely village after your sunbathing session and savor delicious seafood at a waterfront restaurant.

Bitez Beach: Bustle and bliss collide at Bitez, where families build sandcastles, water sports enthusiasts test their mettle, and lively beach bars keep the celebration going into the night.
Address: Bitez Mahallesi, Bodrum 48200, Turkey.
Pricing: Free access, with beach chair and umbrella rentals available.
Tip: Try parasailing or jet skiing for an adrenaline rush, then grab a beverage at a beach bar and enjoy the sunset over the Aegean.

Gumbet Beach: Embrace the throbbing excitement of Gumbet, Bodrum's party hub. Sunbathe on gorgeous sands, cool off in blue waters, and dance the night away at bustling beach bars and nightclubs.
Address: Gumbet Mahallesi, Bodrum 48200, Turkey.
Pricing: Free access, with beach chair and umbrella rentals available.
Tip: Be prepared for crowds and strong feelings, especially during peak season.

Water Sports for the Thrill Seekers:

Windsurfing: Catch the Aegean breeze at Yalıkavak Bay, a windsurfing paradise with dedicated schools and equipment rentals.

Scuba Diving: Explore the underwater world off Bodrum's shore, marveling at vivid coral reefs and schools of fish. Several dive centers provide beginner-friendly tours and lessons.

Kayaking: Paddle along the gorgeous coastline, exploring hidden coves and enjoying the calm of the water. Kayak rentals are available at most beaches.

Hidden Coves for Paradise Hunters

Akvaryum Koyu: Tucked away near Gümüşlük, this isolated cove features crystalline waters and soft rocks, perfect for a serene vacation.
Address: Akvaryum Koyu, Bodrum 48200, Turkey.
Pricing: Free admittance.
Tip: Access the cove by a short walk from the main road.

Camel Bay: Hike down a steep trail to find this hidden treasure near Gümbet. Crystal-clear seas and steep cliffs offer a breathtaking location for leisure and snorkeling.
Address: Camel Bay, Bodrum 48200, Turkey.
Pricing: Free admittance.
Tip: Pack sturdy shoes for the hike and bring your own snacks and drinks.

Kızılbuk: Enjoy the calm of this little cove near Yalıkavak, with blue waves lapping against a backdrop of thick flora. Ideal for snorkeling and soaking up the sun in peace.
Address: Kızılbuk Koyu, Bodrum 48200, Turkey.
Pricing: Free admittance.
Tip: Bring your own beach towels and shade as there are few amenities.

Bonus Tips for First-Timers:
- Research beach facilities and amenities before you go.
-Pack water shoes for rocky coves and uneven terrain.
- Respect the local ecosystem and leave no trace behind.
- Be mindful of currents and water conditions, especially while swimming with children.
- Embrace the diversity of Bodrum's beaches and experience them all!

So, take your sunhat, a feeling of adventure, and let Bodrum's vibrant beaches weave their magic on your first-time journey. Whether you prefer sun-kissed leisure, exhilarating water sports, or the isolated beauty of secret coves, Bodrum offers a magnificent stretch of sand waiting to be discovered. Happy beach hopping fellow explorer!

CHAPTER 7:

GASTRONOMIC ADVENTURES

Bodrum Bonanza: A Gastronomic Adventure for First-Timers

Bodrum's beauty isn't just confined to sun-kissed beaches and ancient ruins; its culinary scene is a colorful ballet of flavors and scents waiting to tickle your taste senses. From savory meze platters to melt-in-your-mouth baklava, get ready to embark on a delightful tour through Bodrum's gourmet treasures!

Authentic Turkish Cuisine:

The Meze Marvel: Dive into the realm of petite, savory dishes that are the cornerstone of Turkish dining. Sample grilled vegetables, dolmas (stuffed grape leaves), creamy dips like hummus and muhammara, and fresh seafood treats like calamari and shrimp.
Price: Expect to pay around 20-40 TRY each dish (around $2.50-$5 USD).

Kebabs for Kings: From succulent Adana kebabs (spicy minced beef skewers) to juicy Iskender kebabs (thinly sliced lamb served with yogurt and tomato sauce), kebabs are a must-try in Bodrum. Don't forget to serve them with crispy pide (flatbread) and a splash of fresh lemon. **Price**: Kebabs cost from 30-50 TRY (roughly $4-$6 USD) depending on the variety and location.

Seafood Sensations: Bodrum's seaside setting offers plenty of fresh seafood. Indulge in grilled octopus, pan-fried calamari, or delicate grilled seafood direct from the Aegean Sea.
Price: Fresh fish varies depending on the catch, but expect to pay roughly 50-80 TRY (around $6-$10 USD) for each dish.

Street Food Gems:

Simit Bliss: No Turkish gourmet excursion is complete without trying simit, a circular sesame-covered bread ring. Grab one for breakfast, a quick snack, or as a wonderful souvenir.
Price: Simit is relatively economical, costing roughly 2-3 TRY (around $0.25-$0.40 USD) per.

Döner Delight: Experience the legendary döner kebabs, slow-cooked meat sliced from a revolving spit and wrapped in warm pita bread. Choose from chicken,

lamb, or beef, then add toppings like fresh vegetables, yogurt, and spicy sauce.
Price: Döner wraps are budget-friendly, costing roughly 15-20 TRY (approximately $2-$2.50 USD) per.

Gözleme Goodness: Warm, delicious gözleme are like Turkish flatbreads loaded with numerous delights. Try the spinach and feta combination, the potato and onion traditional, or even a sweet dessert variation loaded with honey and walnuts.
Price: Gözleme is another budget-friendly choice, costing roughly 10-15 TRY (approximately $1-$1.50 USD) per.

Bonus Tips for First-Time Travelers:
Venture beyond the tourist traps: Head to local eateries and street vendors for authentic flavors and reduced prices.
Don't be scared to try new things: Ask for recommendations and embrace the adventurous spirit of Turkish food.
Learn basic Turkish phrases: "Teşekkür ederim" (thank you) and "Afiyet olsun" (enjoy your meal) go a long way.
Carry cash: Some smaller vendors and street food stalls do not accept cards.
Bring your appetite: Turkish quantities are frequently generous, so come prepared to share and relish the tastes.

Here are some resources to help you explore Bodrum's culinary scene:

TripAdvisor: Find reviews and recommendations for restaurants in Bodrum.

Yelp: Discover local favorites and hidden gems.

Bodrum Peninsula Travel Guide: Explore articles and recommendations for eating in Bodrum.

Taste of Bodrum: A food blog with recipes and insights into Bodrum's cuisine.

Ready to embark on a delightful journey? Get your taste buds primed and dive into the lively world of Bodrum's gourmet delights!

Best Local Restaurants

The culinary scene in Bodrum is bursting with flavor, offering a variety of treats that include fresh seafood, traditional Turkish delicacies, and a dash of cosmopolitan flair. Immerse yourself in these varied dining experiences:

The town of Gemibaşı, located in Bodrum:

The local octopus, luscious mussels, and fisherman's stew are just some of the legendary delicacies that can be enjoyed in this picturesque location with views of the ocean.

Address: Çarşı Mahallesi, Neyzen Tevfik Street, Number 5, Bodrum 48400, Turkey.

Website:
[https://www.tripadvisor.com/Restaurant_Review-g298658-d3343574-Reviews-Gemibasi_Restaurant-Bodrum_City_Bodrum_District_Mugla_Province_Turkish_Aegean_Coa.html]

Price: (expect $50-80 per person)

Tip: Make reservations, especially during peak season.

In the city of Gumusluk, Naru Bodrum:

Mediterranean fusion: This cuisine has dishes that are exquisitely presented and combine regional ingredients with Italian and Greek influences. Enjoy beautiful sunset views from the terrace.

Address: Gümüşlük Koyu, Bodrum 48200, Turkey.

Website:
[https://www.instagram.com/narubodrum/?hl=en]

Phone: +90 252 456 65 65

Price: $30-50 per person

Tip: Dress for a sophisticated ambience.

Ada Beach Restaurant, Gündoğan:

Beachside bliss: Dine with your toes on the sand, enjoying fresh seafood meze platters and grilled favorites. Relax with beverages as the sun dips into the Aegean.
Address: Gündoğan Mahallesi, Bodrum 48200, Turkey.
Website:
https://m.facebook.com/pages/category/async/restaurant/?page=2)
Price: $30-50 per person
Note: Arrive early to grab a beachfront table.

Bonus Tip: Don't be hesitant to eat street food! Sample gözleme (savory flatbreads), simit (sesame bagels), and fresh fruit from local markets.

Note this, Bodrum's gastronomic map is broad and ever-evolving. Be adventurous, ask locals for recommendations, and appreciate the diverse flavors that Bodrum has to offer! Happy dining!

CHAPTER 8:

VIBRANT NIGHTLIFE

Bodrum Beats: Nightlife Hotspots for First-Timers

Bodrum's nightlife pulsates with vitality, offering something for every groove. Here's a quick guide to two contrasting scenes:

Beach Clubs & Bars:

Maçakızı: Soak up sunset views at this legendary beach club, with DJs spinning house tunes, fire shows, and VIP cabanas. Expect tremendous energy and a party mood.
Price: Cover charge varies, beverages about €15-€20.
Website: [https://www.macakizi.com/]

Gumbet Strip: Dive into the center of Bodrum's party scene, with bars lining the shore, offering live music, DJs, and dancing till dawn.
Price: Affordable beverages, roughly €5-€10.
Location: Gumbet Beach

Traditional Turkish Music Venues:

Hasır Restaurant: Experience the beauty of Turkish music at this quaint restaurant with live performances by many musicians, singers, and dancers. Enjoy wonderful Turkish cuisine beside the music.
Price: Dinner and performance roughly €30-€40.
Address: Cumhuriyet Mahallesi, Barlar Sokak No: 10, 48400 Bodrum, Turkey.
Phone: +90 252 316 15 16

Karaoke Bars: Belt out your favorite tunes at one of Bodrum's many karaoke bars. A fun and participatory way to discover Turkish culture and nightlife.
Price: Entry free, drinks approximately €5-€10.
Locations: Scattered around Bodrum town and Gumbet.

Tips for First-Timers:
- Dress comfortably for dancing and late-night adventures.
- Be aware of drink pricing, especially at beach clubs.
- Learn a few basic Turkish words to wow the locals.
- Use licensed taxis or organize transportation prior.
- Most importantly, relax, have fun, and enjoy the dynamic energy of Bodrum nightlife!

Bodrum After Dark: Dazzling Night Markets and Bustling Bazaars

Bodrum comes alive as the sun dips below the horizon. Dive into the vivid tapestry of its nightlife with these intriguing night markets and bazaars:

Bodrum Grand Bazaar:

A shopper's paradise: From gorgeous carpets and hand-painted ceramics to dazzling jewelry and scented spices, bargain your way through a maze of stalls filled with Turkish treasures.
Location: Cumhuriyet Mahallesi, Neyzen Tevfik Cd. No:3 Bodrum 48400, Turkey
Open: Open daily until midnight, busiest evenings and weekends.
Tip: Bring your bargaining skills and cash for the greatest discounts.

Yalıkavak Akça Bazaar:

Boutique bonanza: Discover unique handcrafted jewelry, fashionable apparel, and homeware from local artisans. Sip on fresh lemonade while meandering through the lovely, lantern-lit lanes.
Location: Yalıkavak Mahallesi, Bodrum 48400, Turkey

Open: Open daily till midnight, busiest during summer months.
Tip: Look for one-of-a-kind artifacts and enjoy the casual atmosphere.

Gumbet Bar Street:

Party central: Bustling with neon lights and pounding music, this colorful strip provides a choice of bars, clubs, and live music venues appealing to all tastes.
Location: Gumbet Mahallesi, Bodrum 48400, Turkey
Open: Bars open late, clubs normally open after midnight.
Tip: Dress to impress and prepare for a vibrant scene.

Bonus Tip: Don't forget to eat wonderful street cuisine while touring the markets. Grilled kebabs, gözleme (flatbreads), and simit (bagels) are famous local favorites.

Bodrum's nightlife scene caters to all moods, from immersive shopping experiences to thrilling parties. Choose your journey and prepare to be astonished by the lively after-dark energy of this Turkish paradise.

CHAPTER 9:

WELLNESS AND RELAXATION

Bodrum Bliss: Unwind and Rejuvenate

Beyond the beaches and bazaars, Bodrum offers a refuge for relaxation and wellness. Pamper yourself with these revitalizing experiences:

Turkish Baths and Spas:

Indulge in a classic hammam: Experience the purifying routine of a Turkish bath, with steam rooms, exfoliating scrubs, and calming massages.
Sultan Spa: Luxurious hammam experience with marble interiors and an array of massages.
Prices start at €40 for a simple hammam, and €80 for hammam with massage.
Website:
https://www.instagram.com/sultan_hamam_/?hl=en

Çeşme Hamam: Authentic hammam giving traditional treatments at cheap costs.
 Prices start at ₺200 for a basic hammam.
Phone: +90 252 313 42 09

Yoga Retreats:

Find your inner peace: Immerse yourself in yoga, meditation, and wellness courses at a dedicated retreat center.
Nirvana Yoga Retreat: Offers seaside yoga retreats with various packages and activities.
Prices start at €500 per person for a weekend retreat.
Website: [https://www.nirvanarak.com/booking-engine]

Aura Yoga Center: Hosts yoga retreats and lessons in a lovely mountain environment near Bodrum.
Prices start at ₺800 per person for a weekend retreat.
Phone: +90 252 316 25 15

Bonus Tips:
Book appointments in advance: Popular spas and retreats fill up quickly, especially during peak season.
Dress comfortably: Loose clothing is advised for both hammams and yoga.
Bring water and snacks: Some retreats and hammams may not have easily available food and drinks.
Respect local customs: Be cautious of modest clothes and decorum among spas and retreat centers.

Unwind, relax, and reconnect with yourself in Bodrum's quiet havens. Let these health experiences nourish your body and soul, leaving you feeling renewed and ready to embrace the adventures ahead.

Bodrum Bliss: Unwind at Top Wellness Resorts for First-Timers

Bodrum's sunlight beckons, but relaxation goes beyond beach laziness. Discover serenity at these best wellness resorts, suitable for first-time tourists seeking rejuvenation:

1. The LifeCo Bodrum:
Detox and revitalize with individualized programs concentrating on weight management, chronic disease management, and overall well being. Luxurious facilities include saunas, hammams, and an infinity pool overlooking the Aegean.
Website:
[https://www.thelifeco.com/en/centers/the-lifeco-bodrum-wellness-retreat/]
Pricing: Programs start from €3,200 (roughly $3,400 USD) per week
Contact: +90 252 311 05 40

2. Six Senses Kaplankaya:
Indulge in holistic health with individualized detox, sleep, and anti-aging programs offered by skilled

practitioners. Breathtaking cliffside setting with infinity pools, yoga studios, and a state-of-the-art wellness facility.

Website:
[https://www.sixsenses.com/en/resorts/kaplankaya]

Pricing: Programs start from €4,000 (roughly $4,200 USD) per week

Contact: +90 252 356 00 00

3. Caresse, a Luxury Collection Resort & Spa: Experience a blend of luxury and relaxation with rejuvenating spa treatments, yoga lessons, and a fitness facility. Relax by the infinity pool or private beach after indulging in excellent meals.

Website:
[https://www.marriott.com/en-us/hotels/bjvlc-caresse-a-luxury-collection-resort-and-spa-bodrum/overview/]

Pricing: Rooms start from €250 (roughly $260 USD) per night, spa treatments and wellness programs at additional cost

Contact: +90 252 311 36 36

Bonus Tip: Book your stay in advance, especially during high season, to assure availability.

CHAPTER 10:

DAY TRIPS AND EXCURSIONS

Ephesus Day Trip & Pamukkale Excursion

Bodrum isn't only beaches and bazaars! Venture beyond the town with these fascinating day trips:

Ephesus Day Trip:

Journey through history: Explore the ruins of an ancient Greek and Roman city, once a significant harbor and center of worship. Marvel at the Library of Celsus, Temple of Hadrian, and the Great Theater.
Travel options: Organized tours by bus or boat, solo travel by bus or train.
Time commitment: Day trip (full day).
Tips: Wear comfortable shoes for walking, carry sunscreen and a hat.

Pamukkale Excursion:

Natural wonder: Witness the "Cotton Castle" — cascading white terraces of mineral pools formed by hot springs. Take a plunge at the Cleopatra Pool (optional).

Travel options: Organized excursions by bus, solo travel by bus or train (longer route).
Time commitment: Day trip (whole day).
Tips: Bring swimwear and towels, wear water shoes for the terraces.

Bonus Tip: Combine Ephesus with Pamukkale for a jam-packed historical and ecological excursion!

Note, research tour options and booking details in advance to ensure a seamless and unforgettable excursion.

So, bring your spirit of adventure and prepare to be astounded by Bodrum's hidden delights beyond the beach!

Island Hopping & Nature's Enchantment

Island Hopping:

Kos Island, Greece: Ferry your way to historic wonders like the Asclepion and Castle of the Knights, feast in Greek cuisine, and sunbathe on gorgeous beaches. Hop

aboard a hydrofoil (20 mins) or normal ferry (45 mins) from Bodrum harbor.
Cost: €50-€80 return.

Nature's Enchantment:

Dalyan River Cruise: Glide through a picturesque stream, marvel at mud baths and old rock tombs cut into cliffs, and observe loggerhead turtles sunning themselves. Depart from Bodrum by bus or ferry.
Cost: €50-€80 including transportation and lunch.

Bonus Tip: Combine your Dalyan adventure with a visit to Ephesus, an awe-inspiring UNESCO World Heritage Site, for a full day of historical immersion.

These day tours offer a taste of Greece's charm and Turkey's natural beauty, expanding your Bodrum experience.

CHAPTER 11:

SHOPPING EXTRAVAGANZA

Bodrum Bazaar Bonanza: Shopping Tips for Treasure Hunters

Grand Bazaar:

Address: Neyzen Tevfik Sk No:8, Gumbet Mahallesi, 48400 Bodrum/Muğla, Turkey **Website**: None, but check travel blogs for photographs and insights.
Pricing: Haggling is expected! Start with 50% of the asking price and work your way up.
Tips: Get lost in the maze passageways, peruse leather products, fabrics, jewelry, and spices. Pack your patience and sense of humor for a pleasant haggling session.

Local Handicrafts and Souvenirs:

Bodrum Marina: Find unusual souvenir shops selling pottery plates, evil eye talismans, and handcrafted jewelry.
Yalıkavak: Discover art galleries and boutiques showcasing locally crafted textiles, leather bags, and home furnishings.

Gümüşlük: Explore quaint shops providing embroidered linens, handmade soaps, and distinctive pottery.

Tips: Support local craftspeople! Look for quality materials and innovative designs. Don't be hesitant to ask about the meaning and traditions of the crafts.

Bonus Tip: Pack an empty suitcase! You'll uncover enticing gifts at every step.

Remember, shopping in Bodrum is an adventure, not just a transaction. Embrace the experience, enjoy the vibrant environment, and discover unique treasures to remind you of your Turkish voyage.

Bodrum Boutique Bonanza: Chic Shopping Districts for First-Timers

Bodrum isn't only beaches and history; it's a shopper's paradise! Dive into these bustling districts and unearth unique treasures:

1. Cumhuriyet Caddesi, Bodrum Town:

Local flair meets trendy: Explore art galleries, independent boutiques, and souvenir shops filled with artisan jewelry, textiles, and ceramics.

Address: Cumhuriyet Caddesi, Bodrum 48200, Turkey
Tip: Bargain like a pro! Most shops allow bartering, especially for textiles and souvenirs.

2. Yalıkavak Marina:

premium on the waterfront: Browse designer boutiques featuring worldwide brands, premium jewelry, and gorgeous homeware.
Website: [https://www.yalikavakmarina.com/]
Tip: Enjoy a luxurious lunch or sunset cocktails after your shopping adventure.

3. Türkbükü Boardwalk:

Bohemian chic by the beach: Discover contemporary beachwear shops, boho-inspired apparel businesses, and local craftsmen selling handmade products.
Address: Türkbükü Mahallesi, Bodrum 48200, Turkey
Tip: Combine shopping with a great seafood meal at a beachfront restaurant.

Bonus Tip: Download the "Kent Kart" app for public transit discounts and access to shopping specials.

Note this down, with a grin, some Turkish, and your bargaining skills on point, you'll discover treasures and memories to last a lifetime in Bodrum!

CHAPTER 12:

ACCOMMODATION GUIDE

Bodrum Luxury Retreats: Sun-Kissed Splendor for First-Time Visitors

Bodrum's allure goes beyond the beaches; it unfolds in opulent havens created for maximum indulgence. Dive into these best resorts for a first-hand experience of soothing paradise:

1. Caresse, a Luxury Collection Resort & Spa in Bodrum:

Address: Asarlik Mevkii, Adnan Menderes Cd. No. 89, Bodrum 48200, Turkey.
Website:
[https://www.marriott.com/en-us/hotels/bjvlc-caresse-a-luxury-collection-resort-and-spa-bodrum/overview/]
Phone: +90 252 311 36 36
Check-in/out times: 3PM/12PM
Price: €400+ per night
Details: Private beach, infinity pool, world-class spa, excellent cuisine, and breathtaking Aegean views.

2. Six Senses Kaplankaya :

Address: Kaplankaya Mevkii, Bodrum 48200, Turkey.
Website:
[https://www.sixsenses.com/en/resorts/kaplankaya]
Phone number: +90 252 356 00 00
Check-in and check-out times: 3PM and 12PM.
Price: €800+ per night
Features: Cliffside location, infinity pools, award-winning spa, individualized wellness programs, gourmet cuisine.

3. Mandarin Oriental in Bodrum:
Address: Cennet Koyu Mevkii, Bodrum, 48200, Turkey.
Website: [https://www.mandarinoriental.com/bodrum/]
Phone number: +90 252 511 40 00.
Check-in and check-out times: 3PM and 12PM.Price: €600 or more per night.
Details: Private beach with breathtaking views of the Aegean, a magnificent hammam, award-winning restaurants, and a children's club.

Tip for First-Timers: Book early, especially during high season, to ensure your preferred dates and avoid disappointment.

Keep in mind that these are only a few of the premium options available in Bodrum. When making your decision, keep your budget in mind, as well as the resort atmosphere you want. Immerse yourself in the luxurious luxury and exquisite service that these resorts provide, and make wonderful moments in Bodrum.

Bodrum Budget Bonanza: Cozy Stays without Breaking the Bank

Bodrum's charm extends beyond luxury resorts, offering budget-friendly havens for first-time adventurers. Here are a few snug gems to consider:

1. Merhaba Hotel, Bodrum Town:

Location: Central, walking distance to major sites and nightlife.
Vibe: Basic but clean rooms, pleasant atmosphere, rooftop patio with sea views.
Price: €25-€40 per night (double room)
Website: [https://merhabaotel.com/]
Phone: +90 533 161 26 45.
Check-in/out: 2pm/12pm.
Tip: Book in advance during the high season.

2. New Bodrum Hotel, Bodrum Town:

Location: Near Bodrum Castle, accessible to public transportation and shops.

Vibe: Modern and comfortable rooms, rooftop pool with great views.
Price: €30-€50 per night (double room).
Website: [https://newbodrumhotel.com/]
Phone: +90 252 319 53 93.
Check-in/out: 2pm/12pm.
Tip: Request a room with a castle view.

3. MİA BUTİK OTEL, Bodrum Town:

Location: Quiet street near the marina, gorgeous castle views.
Vibe: Charming boutique hotel with unique Turkish design, rooftop patio with jacuzzi.
Price: €40-€60 per night (double room).
Website: [http://miabutikotel.eatbu.com/]
 Phone: +90 542 815 41 48.
Check-in/out: 2pm/12pm.
Tip: Enjoy their wonderful complimentary breakfast on the rooftop.

Bonus Tip: Consider staying away from the main tourist regions for even better deals. Look for guesthouses or family-run hotels for a more authentic Turkish experience.

Have it in mind, budget-friendly doesn't mean compromising on comfort or location. With a bit of study, you can find a snug refuge that matches your needs and lets you enjoy Bodrum's beauty without breaking the wallet. Happy travels!

Bodrum Beyond the Ordinary: Unique Airbnb Stays for First-Timers

Forget conventional hotels and immerse yourself in the essence of Bodrum with these amazing Airbnb gems:

1. Traditional Stone House in Gümüşlük:

Live like a local: This beautiful stone cottage offers stunning sea views, a private terrace, and a flavor of classic Turkish architecture.
Address: Gümüşlük Koyu, Bodrum 48200, Turkey.
Website:
[https://www.airbnb.com/gumusluk-turkiye/stays]
Price: $120-$150 each night.
Check-in/out: Flexible self check-in/out with keyless entry.
Tip: Enjoy delicious seafood at neighboring restaurants and discover the lovely village of Gümüşlük.

2. Cave House with Panoramic Views:

Cliffside living: Experience amazing panoramic views from this unusual cave house, including a private pool and a pleasant interior.

Address: Akyarlar Mahallesi, Bodrum 48200, Turkey.

Website:
[https://www.airbnb.com/bodrum-turkiye/stays]

Price: $200-$250 per night.

Check-in/out: Flexible self check-in/out with keyless entry.

Tip: Take a plunge in the infinity pool and watch the sunset paint the Aegean sky.

3. Luxury Treehouse in Yalıkavak:

Sleep amongst the leaves: This magnificent treehouse hidden in a verdant garden offers a unique hideaway with a private balcony and a treetop terrace.

Address: Yalıkavak Mahallesi, Bodrum 48200, Turkey.

Website:
[https://www.airbnb.com/yalikavak-turkiye/stays]

Price: $150-$200 per night.

Check-in/out: Flexible self check-in/out with keyless entry.

Tip: Combine your stay with a visit to the magnificent Yalıkavak Marina and its luxury retailers.

Bonus Tip: Read reviews carefully, ask questions to the host, and book well in advance, especially during high season.

Embrace Bodrum's spirit of adventure and choose an Airbnb that suits your individual travel style.

CHAPTER 13:

LOCAL TIPS AND INSIGHTS

Insider Recommendations

Forget the tourist traps, first-timers! Bodrum holds secrets beyond the beaches and bazaars, waiting to be opened by those who dare to step off the main route. So, abandon the guidebooks and follow these insider recommendations to experience the genuine Bodrum like a local:

Food for the Soul:

Ditch the tourist port restaurants: Head to Kumluk village for the freshest seafood at Mehmet Usta Bodrum Balıkçısı. Watch the sun dip over the bay as you devour grilled octopus and meze platters.
Fuel your day with a Simit: Skip the hotel buffet and get a Simit, a sesame-encrusted bread ring, from a local bakery. Pair it with Turkish tea for a wonderful and cheap breakfast.
Hidden gem alert: For the tastiest gözleme (savory flatbread) in Bodrum, head to Gümüşlük's Körfez Restaurant. Their spinach and feta stuffing is legendary, and the sunset views are incomparable.

Beyond the Beach:

Hike the Bodrum Peninsula: Lace up your boots and conquer the picturesque Kalamaki or Güllük routes. Breathe in the fresh air, bask in the panoramic vistas, and uncover secret coves suitable for a refreshing plunge.
Unleash your inner archaeologist: Explore the ancient city of Myndos, set on a rock overlooking the Aegean. Get lost in the ruins of temples, theaters, and agoras, and picture the glory days of this ancient civilization.
Kayak through Paradise Bay: Rent a kayak and paddle through the blue waters of Paradise Bay. Discover quiet coves, encounter playful dolphins, and appreciate the breathtaking natural beauty of Bodrum's coastline.

Nightlife with a Twist:

Sip cocktails under the stars: Leave the busy bars behind and head to Dukkan Bodrum. This rooftop bar provides amazing views, inventive cocktails, and a refined setting without the pretentiousness.
Live music at its best: Catch a local band at Maça Bodrum. This hidden gem buried away in a side street features a relaxing attitude, friendly residents, and music that will have your feet dancing.
Belly dancing like a pro: Learn the art of belly dance at one of the numerous local studios. Unleash your inner

dancer, engage with the local culture, and have a lot of fun in the process.

Cultural Immersion:

Haggle in the bazaar: Embrace the culture of bargaining in the Bodrum Grand Bazaar. Don't be afraid to smile, joke, and make an offer - it's all part of the fun!
Visit the local markets: Go beyond the souvenirs and experience the genuine Bodrum at the Güllük or Gümüşlük markets. Sample regional cuisines, interact with friendly sellers, and experience the pulse of daily life.
Take a Turkish bath: Pamper yourself with a traditional hammam experience. Soak in steaming chambers, get pampered with a cleanse and massage, and emerge feeling renewed and invigorated.

Bonus Tip: Learn a few basic Turkish phrases like "Merhaba" (hello), "Teşekkür ederim" (thank you), and "Afiyet olsun" (enjoy your dinner). It goes a long way in interacting with the people and boosting your experience.

So, first-timers, skip the itinerary and accept the unexpected. Let these insider tips be your compass, travel with curiosity, and discover the Bodrum that exists beyond the guidebooks. Remember, the most real experiences are frequently discovered on the side streets, in the hidden gems, and in the hearts of the local people. Now go forth, explore, and paint your own unforgettable Bodrum masterpiece!

Off-the-Beaten-Path Experiences

Bodrum may sparkle with sun-kissed beaches and historic antiquities, but for the truly adventurous person, its magic comes in stepping beyond the tourist track. Ditch the guidebooks and embrace the whispering of the wind, because these off-the-beaten-path excursions will paint your Bodrum vacation with brilliant hues of local charm and hidden treasures:

1. Sail into Serenity: Escape the crowds and travel around the rough coastline aboard a classic wooden gulet. Discover isolated coves with turquoise waters, excellent for swimming and snorkeling. Feast on delicious seafood prepared onboard while the captain regales you with tales of the Aegean. Embark from Bodrum Harbor or lovely Gümüşlük village.

2. Hike the Bozdag Peninsula: Lace up your boots and hike through the green Bozdag Peninsula, a sanctuary for wild orchids, olive groves, and ancient ruins. Follow the perfumed mountain pathways, passing small communities and spectacular landscapes. Reward yourself with a plunge in the crystal-clear waters of Cleopatra Beach or a traditional meal at a secret highland taverna.

3. Unearth History at Pedasa: Step back in time at the lost city of Pedasa, situated between rolling hills. Explore the relics of temples, theaters, and aqueducts, whispering stories of a once-thriving society. Climb to the acropolis for panoramic views, and imagine the echoes of chariot racing in the old stadium.

4. Unwind in Turgutreis: Trade the tourist hubbub for the laid-back appeal of Turgutreis. Stroll around the tiny lanes lined with colorful buildings, sip Turkish coffee with the locals, and bargain for handmade goods at the vibrant market. Enjoy excellent seafood near the harbor or bask on the private beach, far from the Bodrum crowds.

5. Discover Secret Waterfalls: Follow the hidden roads near Güllük Bay and stumble upon flowing waterfalls, hidden oasis-like havens within the beautiful hills. Swim in the calm waters, soak up the sun on the granite ledges, and let the soft spray sing you. These refreshing hideaways are the perfect retreat from the summer heat.

6. Dive into History at Bardakci Bay: Slip into the turquoise waters of Bardakci Bay and discover a treasure mine of underwater history. Explore antique amphorae, shipwrecks, and colorful aquatic life amidst the coral reefs. A certified diving experience will uncover a hidden world of enchantment beneath the Aegean waters.

7. Kayak to Rabbit Island: Paddle your way to the tiny isle of Tavşan Adası (Rabbit Island) off the coast of Güllük. Explore the ancient ruins, swim in the crystal-clear waters, and soak up the sun on the pristine beach. A really off-the-beaten-path sanctuary, accessible only by boat or kayak.

8. Join a Local Cooking Class: Immerse yourself in Turkish culinary culture by participating in a traditional cooking lesson. Learn the secrets of local foods including meze platters, fresh fish grills, and melt-in-your-mouth baklava. Savor your creations with renewed respect for the vivid tastes of Bodrum cuisine.

9. Experience a Turkish Hammam: Rejuvenate your body and soul with a visit to a traditional Turkish hammam. Soak in the warm tubs, have a thorough scrub, and emerge feeling cleansed and pampered. A centuries-old ritual that will leave you feeling refreshed and involved in local wellness traditions.

10. Hike the Ancient Silk Road: Follow the footprints of caravans on the Bodrum stretch of the old Silk Road. Trek through olive trees and pomegranate orchards, passing Ottoman caravanserais and historical sites. This trip through time connects you with the rich legacy of the region.

Local Tips:
Rent a scooter or bicycle: Explore the tiny villages and secret coves at your own pace.
Learn some basic Turkish phrases: It goes a long way in interacting with the people and boosting your experience.
Support local businesses: Choose family-run shops and eateries for authentic experiences and unusual finds.
Respect local customs: Dress modestly while visiting religious sites and be sensitive to cultural norms.
Embrace the unexpected: Leave your itinerary loose and be open to discovering hidden gems along the road.

Put in mind, the most gratifying travel experiences often lie beyond the mainstream. So, bring your spirit of adventure, a dash of curiosity, and get ready to reveal the hidden wonders of Bodrum. Let the wind whisper its secrets, the villagers tell their stories, and your own feet guide you on an adventure you'll never forget. Happy exploring!

Bodrum Babble: Cracking the Language Code for First-Timers

While magnificent beaches and historic ruins may attract you to Bodrum, navigating the vibrant terrain can be easier with a dash of Turkish! Don't worry, first-timer, you don't need to become a linguist, but mastering a few basic phrases will unlock smiles, boost confidence, and improve your Bodrum experience. So, bundle your curiosity and let's dig into some crucial Turkish facts!

Greetings and Politeness:

Merhaba: Hello (global greeting)
Günaydın: Good morning
İyi akşamlar: Good evening
Nasılsınız?: How are you? (formal)
İyiyim, teşekkür ederim: I'm good, thank you (formal)
Sağ olun: Thank you (informal)
Lütfen: Please
Rica ederim: You're welcome

Asking Questions:

Ne kadar?: How much?
Burası neresi?: Where is this?

Tuvalet nerede?: Where is the restroom?
Hesap lütfen: Check, please
İngilizce konuşuyor musunuz?: Do you speak English?

Numbers and Basics:

Bir: One, **İki**: Two, **Üç**: Three, **Dört**: Four, **Beş**: Five, **Evet**: Yes, **Hayır**: No, **Su**: Water, **Kahve**: Coffee, **Çay**: Tea, **Tamam**: Okay

Bonus Tips:
Grin and Body linguistic: A warm grin and gestures go a long way in bridging linguistic problems.
Learn the Turkish Alphabet: Basic pronunciation can assist in interpreting signs and menus.
Download Translator Apps: Use apps like Google Translate for instant assistance.
Don't Be Afraid to Make Mistakes: Locals appreciate the effort, even if your Turkish isn't perfect.
Have Fun! Language learning should be a joyful experience, so relax and accept the process.

Note, even a few basic phrases can open doors, make connections, and enrich your Bodrum journey. So, take a deep breath, say "Merhaba" with confidence, and let the language of Turkish hospitality weave its magic on your vacation!

Pro Tip: Learn the Turkish phrase "Afiyet olsun," which means "Enjoy your meal." It's a guaranteed way to wow locals at restaurants and markets!

CHAPTER 14:

PRACTICAL INFORMATION

Emergency Contacts

General Emergencies:

Emergency Phone Number: 112 (reaches police, fire department, and ambulance)

Turkish Red Crescent: +90 252 241 41 41
 (provides first aid and emergency medical assistance)
Bodrum State Hospital: +90 252 414 12 81 (provides complete medical care)

Police:
For general police assistance, contact the Bodrum Gendarmerie Command at +90 252 414 10 10.
For tourist-related matters, contact the Bodrum Tourist Police at +90 252 414 02 70.

Foreign Embassies:

US Embassy Ankara: +90 312 457 7000
UK Embassy Ankara: +90 312 457 2700
Canadian Embassy Ankara: +90 312 457 2400

Useful numbers:

Airport Information: +90 252 479 49 49 (Milas-Bodrum Airport)
Taxi Dispatch: +90 252 414 14 14 (Bodrum)
Tourism Information: +90 252 414 15 15 (Bodrum).

Additional Tip:
-Before you travel, save these numbers to your phone.
-Note the address of your hotel/accommodation for future reference.
-Learn simple Turkish phrases such as "help" and "emergency".
-Purchase travel insurance before your journey to ensure peace of mind.
-Remain, be alert of your surroundings and trust your instincts.

Put in mind that safety comes first in your trips. Don't be afraid to seek assistance if necessary. Being prepared and knowledgeable will ensure a safe and happy time in Bodrum.

Please be aware that these are the most general contact numbers available. Information for emergencies on specific islands or in remote places may differ. It is essential that you double-check contact information closer to your trip date or upon arrival in Bodrum.

Health and Safety Tips

Health and Safety Tips in Bodrum for First-Time Visitors:

1. Water: Stick with bottled or purified water. Avoid using tap water and be cautious with ice in drinks.

2. Sun Protection: The weather in Bodrum can be sunny. Apply sunscreen, wear a hat, and remain hydrated.

3. Medical Facilities: Identify local hospitals and clinics. Bring vital prescriptions and a basic first-aid kit.

4. Food Safety: Enjoy the local cuisine, but be cautious with street food. Choose well-established restaurants.

5. Mosquito Protection: Use insect repellent, particularly in the summer, and consider wearing long sleeves at night.

6. Travel Insurance: Ensure you have comprehensive travel insurance that covers medical emergencies.

7. COVID-19 Precautions: Keep up with local COVID-19 guidelines. Follow the appropriate safety precautions.

8. Emergency numbers: Know the local emergency numbers. Dial 112 for medical assistance.

9. Traffic Safety: Be cautious when crossing the roadway. Traffic may differ from what you are used to.

10. Cultural Sensitivity: Follow local customs and dress modestly, especially in religious or rural places.

Prioritize your well-being, be informed, and embrace local norms to ensure a safe and pleasurable trip to Bodrum.

Money Matters

Are you planning an adventure in Bodrum? Let us navigate the financial side!

Currency:

Turkish Lira (TRY): Before traveling, exchange currency or utilize an ATM. To avoid excessive fees, consider getting a travel card.

Cash: Make sure you have adequate cash on hand for modest purchases and emergencies.

Costs:

Accommodation: Set aside $50-$150 per night for comfortable options. Boutique hotels and luxury resorts cost extra.

Food: Street food and local restaurants are reasonably priced ($5-10 per meal). Fancy restaurants charge more ($20-$50).

Activities: Entry prices for attractions range from $5 to $20. Public transportation is inexpensive ($1 to $2).

Saving Tips:

Public transportation: Buses and dolmuşes are reliable and affordable.

Self-catering: Cook meals at your Airbnb to save money on dining out.

Haggling: Allowable in marketplaces and select stores. Be nice and friendly.

Free activities: Visit beaches, hike coastal paths, and enjoy the atmosphere.

Bonus Tip: Purchase a "KentKart" to receive public transportation discounts and access to shopping offers.

Note that your budget can be flexible! Determine your must-dos and adapt accordingly. Most importantly, see Bodrum's beauties without breaking the bank!

Communication Essentials

Here are practical communication basics for travelers:

1. Learn Basic terms: Familiarize yourself with basic terms in the local language, including greetings, polite expressions, and typical questions.

2. Translation Apps: Download translation apps like Google Translate to assist with language hurdles. Some apps offer offline translation features.

3. Local SIM Card: Consider buying a local SIM card for your phone to have a local number and access mobile data. This is useful for communication and navigation.

4. Wi-Fi Availability: Identify areas with free Wi-Fi, such as hotels, cafes, and public spaces. Utilize Wi-Fi for communication and internet access.

5. Emergency Numbers: Save local emergency numbers, contact information for your country's embassy or consulate, and the nearest hospital in your phone.

6. Offline Maps: Download offline maps before your journey to travel without an internet connection. Apps like Google Maps allow you to save maps for offline use.

7. Cultural Sensitivity: Learn about local customs, gestures, and conventions to ensure polite interactions. Cultural sensitivity increases your whole experience.

8. Transportation Knowledge: Learn fundamental transportation-related phrases, such as asking for directions, verifying fares, and comprehending public transportation announcements.

9. Weather Updates: Stay updated about the weather forecast using weather apps to arrange activities accordingly.

10. Time Zone Awareness: Be aware of the local time zone and alter your schedule accordingly. Set your gadgets to the local time.

11. Public transit Info: Understand the local public transit system, including ticketing, routes, and schedules.

12. clothing Appropriately: Respect local clothing regulations, especially when visiting religious or cultural places. Modesty is often appreciated.

13. Local Customs: Familiarize oneself with local customs, greetings, and social etiquette to navigate social settings with ease.

14. Navigation applications: Use navigation applications to find your way around. These applications generally give walking instructions and details about surrounding attractions.

15. Currency Awareness: Know the local currency, basic exchange rates, and currency symbols. Be cautious when handling money to avoid confusion.

16. Safety terms: Learn safety-related terms, such as asking for aid or identifying an emergency. This can be critical in unforeseen situations.

17. Respectful Photography: Ask for permission before shooting images, especially of locals. Be mindful of cultural sensitivities around photography.

18. Wi-Fi Calling: Explore possibilities for making Wi-Fi calls to stay in touch with family and friends without incurring international calling expenses.

By including these communication requirements into your travel preparations, you'll be well-equipped to traverse other cultures and enjoy a smoother travel experience.

CONCLUSION

Recap of Bodrum's Charm

In the twilight shadows of Bodrum's historic walls and the murmurs of waves caressing its shores, my journey in this enchanting enclave comes to a conclusion. Bodrum, a symphony of turquoise waters and historical whispers, has left an unforgettable impact on my soul. From the sunlight strolls through its beautiful alleys to the whispers of wind at the summit of its stately castle, every moment is a tribute to Bodrum's everlasting allure.

As the lively bazaars and the aroma of spices remain in my recollections, I am reminded that Bodrum is not only a destination; it's a thrilling dance of past and present. The cultural riches, the kindness of its people, and the blue embrace of the Aegean Sea have painted my journey with shades of wonder.

In the heart of Bodrum's appeal, I discovered more than a tourist escapade; I found a sanctuary of stories waiting to be unraveled. So, when I bid farewell to Bodrum's magnetic embrace, I bring with me not just the seashells from its shores but a treasury of tales that will long resound in the corridors of my wanderlust-filled heart. Until we meet again, beloved Bodrum, your charm will continue to beckon, like an ever-enticing beacon leading the way for future adventures.

Encouragement for Future Travelers

As the sun drops below the horizon, painting the Bodrum sky in shades of apricot and amethyst, I find myself sadly bidding adieu to this haven of enchantment. To future travelers, let me craft a tale of encouragement—a whisper from the old stones, the Aegean winds, and the laughter ringing through Bodrum's colorful streets.

In the rhythmic dance of history and modernity, Bodrum offers an invitation to be discovered, to be welcomed by the tales of its cobblestone alleys and the vivacity of its bustling markets. Venture into this coastal symphony where the sea hums stories, and the breeze conveys the promise of unexplored adventures.

Embrace the warmth of Bodrum's sun-kissed friendliness, savor the aromas that dance on your palette, and lose yourself in the maze of its ancient legacy. For every sunset viewed above the castle walls and every wave that caresses the coast leaves a mark on the wanderer's heart.

So, to those yet to go on the voyage that is Bodrum, let the anticipation of discovery be your compass. May the antique wonders and modern joys merge to create a symphony of memories that resound long after your footsteps have faded. As you set sail into the charm of Bodrum, may your journey be as timeless and mesmerizing as the whispers borne by the Aegean breeze. Until then, dream of Bodrum's charm, for your own tale awaits in its embrace. Safe travels, intrepid people!

APPENDICES

Useful Phrases in Turkish

1. Greetings:
Hello: Merhaba
Good morning: Günaydın
Good evening: İyi akşamlar
Goodbye: Hoşça kal

2. Politeness:
Please: Lütfen
Thank you: Teşekkür ederim
Excuse me: Affedersiniz
Sorry: Özür dilerim

3. Basic Conversations:
  Yes: Evet - **No**: Hayır
  What is your name?: Adınız nedir?
  My name is...: Adım...

4. Directions:
  - **Where is...?**: ... nerede?
  - **Right**: Sağ , **Left**: Sol
  - **Straight ahead**: Düz git

5. Numbers: **1**: Bir , **2**: İki , **3**: Üç - **10**: On , **100**: Yüz

6. Common Phrases:
  - **I don't understand**: Anlamıyorum
  -**Can you help me**?: Yardım eder misiniz?
  - **How much is this**?: Bu ne kadar?
  - **Where is the bathroom**?: Tuvalet nerede?

7. Dining Out:
  - **Menu**: Menü, Water: Su,
-**Delicious**: Lezzetli
  - **Check, please**: Hesap, lütfen

8. Emergencies:
  Help!: Yardım!
  I need a doctor: Doktora ihtiyacım var - Police: Polis
  Hospital: Hastane

Additional Resources

In addition to the information I've already provided, here are some extra resources that might be helpful for first-time travelers in Bodrum:

Official Websites:

Turkish Ministry of Culture and Tourism:
[https://www.ktb.gov.tr/?_Dil=2]

Provides thorough information on sites, events, transportation, and visas

Bodrum Municipality:
[https://www.bodrum.bel.tr/baskan_ozgecmis]
(Contains local news, events, and information about the community)

Milas-Bodrum Airport:
[https://milas-bodrumairport.com/]
(Offers flight schedules, arrival and departure processes, and airport facilities)

Blogs and Travel Guides:

The Blonde Abroad:
[https://www.theblondeabroad.com/]
(Shares practical advice and recommendations for budget-friendly travel in Bodrum)

Planet Odd:
[https://www.atlasobscura.com/things-to-do/plano-texas]
 (Provides in-depth guides on experiencing Bodrum's historical landmarks and natural beauty)

Nomadic Matt:
[https://www.nomadicmatt.com/] (Offers ideas on saving money while traveling in Turkey, particularly Bodrum)

Apps:

Google Translate:
[https://translate.google.com/]
(Essential for basic communication and comprehending signs)

Duolingo: [https://www.duolingo.com/]
(Learn basic Turkish phrases and vocabulary on the move)

Citymapper: [https://citymapper.com/?lang=en]
(Helps you navigate public transit in Bodrum)

Other Resources:

Bodrum Card:
[https://www.bodrumpeninsulatravelguide.co.uk/kent-card-app-for-the-bodrum-city-bus/] (Offers discounts on attractions, restaurants, and activities)

Turkish Lira Converter:
[https://www.xe.com/currencyconverter/]
(Helps you convert currency and comprehend prices)

Turkey Travel Forum:

[https://www.lonelyplanet.com/landing/lonely-planet-community]
(Connect with other tourists and ask questions about Bodrum)

Do not forget, the greatest resources for your trip will depend on your specific interests and priorities. Do some study and choose the resources that best suit your needs for a terrific first-time experience in Bodrum!

Made in United States
Orlando, FL
05 October 2024